The Ohio State University Press/*The Journal* Award in Poetry

Shadeland
Andrew Grace

The Ohio State University Press
Columbus

Copyright © 2009 by The Ohio State University.
All rights reserved.

Library of Congress Cataloging-in-Publication Data
Grace, Andrew, 1978–
 Shadeland / Andrew Grace.
    p.cm. — (The Ohio State University Press/The Journal Award in Poetry)
ISBN 978-08142-5067-9 (pbk.: alk. paper)
1. Title
PS3607.R325S47 2009
811'.6—dc22

                                    2008025757

This book is available in the following editions:
Paper (ISBN 978-08142-5067-9)
CD-ROM (ISBN 978-08142-9182-5)

Cover design by DesignSmith
Type set in Adobe Granjon
Text design by Juliet Williams

♾ The paper used in this publication meets the minimum requirements of the American National
Standard for Information Sciences—Permanence of Paper for Printed Library Materials. ANSI
Z39.48-1992

9 8 7 6 5 4 3 2 1

In memory of Gary Eugene Grace
June 7, 1951–March 4, 2004

For Tory and Lily

Contents

III.

Acknowledgments

Grateful acknowledgments are made to the editors of the following journals where these poems first appeared, sometimes in earlier versions.

Alembic: "Vantage"
Another Chicago Magazine: "Confession"
Boston Review: "Pilgrim Sonnet," "Pilgrim Sonnet Redux"
Cairn: "Without You, the Meadow," "At Chain of Rocks Canal"
Crab Orchard Review: "At the Outermost Shrine of the Narrowmost Road," "Shadeland"
Denver Quarterly: "Silo," "Of Shade and Body Interwound"
Fourteen Hills: "Prelude to X"
Free Verse: "Curse," "Z"
Gulf Coast: "X"
Harp & Altar: "Of Love and Wild Dogs," "Divisible"
Hayden's Ferry Review: "Achilles in the Heartland," "Invitation"
Indiana Review: "Letter Sent in a Fish," "Letter Sent Back on a Crane's Heel"
Literary Review: "Is to Say"
Ninth Letter: "28th Year"
Southeast Review: "The Imperfect Knowledge of Paolo"
Southern Poetry Review: "For Tityrus"
TYPO: "Dinner for Threshers"
Word For / Word: "Ex Log"
"Descent" was published in *The Human Tentacle* #1.
"Shadeland" was printed as a broadside by the Underwood Poetry Foundation.
"For Tityrus" received the 2003 Guy Owen prize from the *Southern Poetry Review*.

It is an honor to thank the Creative Writing Program at Washington University and the Stegner Program at Stanford University for support and guidance throughout the process of writing this book. Thanks also go to those individuals without whom this book could not have been written: Susan Grace Rominger, Tim Grace, and Paul and Lesley Weber. Deep gratitude goes to Andrew Hudgins for believing in my manuscript. And above all, thanks to Tory.

I.

At Chain of Rocks Canal

Sky's first rung spreads morning's zero draft—
they say a journey is an inch of Hell, maybe two.

Let them find me far from here.
Let them find me in Black Water Lobby, face up, or down.
Let them find me praying in the whining pipes of straw.
Let them find me dumb and thirsting.

I see the road descend.
I see distant silos lit brilliant as Hundred Blossom Tower.
I see the X and O: the unknown and our grief.
I see, and then I do not see, your star.

Invitation

The constellations read like an operator's manual to our reluctant bones:
rise, turn, counterturn, drift, grainout. 1 A.M. black flag and star-grit,
flat clouds, all mauled by wind—this is the sky the earth deserves.

I walk down Route 45, the white spit of weeds clinging to my shoes,
black centralia loam . . . on a pilgrimage it is easier to worship the journey,
but when I hear the burweed's summons, it is You I want to hear.

I am ready to learn the darkness before the light.
Use a golden scalpel, golden stitch.
Last things shining, the O is what I long for, the thorn, the burn.

Achilles in the Heartland

Nineteen horses died beneath you, and yet this one,
black gelding in the pasture where a northerly champs
the gull-colored barley, does not flinch when you reach to it

across our iron fence, shut and rusted purple as a heart, to—
to do what? Master the beast? Mount it, charge the yard raw
and invent real walls to tear down, actual boats to protect?

When wind curves the corn there is a choreography,
like a wave of copper men lowering their faces
to the dust, that can coax blood back into havoc—

for you rage was like drawing a design on a chalkboard.
For us it is like a little light on the water, the odor
of lilac, simple hunger: plain, atmospheric, not to be

avoided or indulged. We live on the plains, discuss
the unseen, know the tang of methamphetamine
being cooked close, somewhere we used to know. A boy,

18, once waited behind our tin shed for all to be dark
and stole the farm truck. It had holes in the floor that would
scroll the hot static of asphalt or packed dirt underfoot.

He made it to Rockford. In his jail cell, before
they even asked us if we wanted to press charges,
he hung himself. The truck was returned and we use it.

Thus our fear: of the negative promise of spring, of lantern light
from deeper in the barn, of sources drying up,
first in the outliers, then in the central, unintelligible

house of belief within us we, in the first place,
feared was still there. Achilles, you are simple. For you
grief metastasizes to rage, which brings revenge,

and that is a type of genius. These cracked acres with last
season's stalks jutting from the dust take you back
to Hector's bones, burnt, brother-sifted from the pyre ashes.

To destroy what you respect, to, once slain, defile it
for ever having been admired, then, to release it
with tenderness into the silvering limbo of your history—

is this the heartbreak of the victor? Our landlords
have sold out as town chews the moth-hole wider, as
black-papered houses, one generation empty, "develop,"

burn. Ours is becoming a country of ex. Sieges born
in chicken blood, Iliads in the off hours, we surrender.
Achilles, if the land offered us any deference,

any gift, we would be Trojans, we would accept, even if it
clinched exile. And when gone, what we'll miss is what
made us never belong: a cracked engine's harried song,

the obscene musk of sick ears of corn, the pigweed's
vermilion post-herbicide scorch, the way the black horse
now seems to us to hunger for your touch, as if it wanted

to be tamed, as if the quake in its side was not the flies,
but the urge to be of use to us, to help us through this hour,
this untilled earth, or any other slow, human Troy.

Pilgrim Sonnet

Beginning with a line from Hopkins

Pilgrims, still pilgrims, still come poor pilgrims,
at night to bring the howling house a door,
the burning man a sigh for his dry soul,
the children rebel poems turned to hymns.

From shrine to shrine, and farm to field, they go
for each of us who sleep in those enormous
ghosts of clothes the wanted-for and to-dust-
relinquished leave behind. They whisper *zero*

is a number too, and dip their hair
in Nameless Creek and shout down to us the way
to follow, one by one and O by O.

But by the morning we have not gone there.
The houses shrill their vowels; the grass quails.
There is no going, or a way to go.

Pilgrim Sonnet Redux

Come poor pilgrims,
There is no shrine, or a way to zero,
Still pilgrims, still pilgrims,
O by shrill and O by quail.

From Nameless Creek to Howling House
Pilgrims go, dry souls, a wanted-for ghost
For each of us who relinquish vowels
Into morning dust, fields turned to hymns.

They shout us down for the way we have not gone there.
They farm burning poems.
They whisper in their rebel sleep.

Poor pilgrims, one by one, come—
The enormous grass is the shrine.
The door is the night you leave behind.

Prelude to X

Say the sky, Atlantic, inviolate,
holds X amount of rescue.

Shallow, in the quiet wind,
the drenched
voice,
do you know me?

And full-on in the bleached grass
your outstretched
need for X to be infinite.

Dinner for Threshers

Grant Wood, oil on hardboard, 1934

1.

Noon. A thresher waits
    to wash the debris from his face into
a stone bowl. His hair is stiff
    with lice. A rooster
       missed its hour, tries
    to scream the sun back down; it is Iowa,
1892. A draft horse the color
    of zinc tongues its own shadow.
The thresher is about to join a table
    of men—fourteen of them, as in the Last Supper—
in the house
    for lunch. The string of Xs
formed by the backs of the men's overalls marks a negation.
    They lift the offering to their
       mouths: blood, flesh;
    coffee, rabbit.

2.

    Their minds are on process:
      thrash, shake, winnow. Two thousand
bushels bagged in a pigeon-crusted loft.
    Two thousand to go.
    Man in the hopper,
  man on the stack of moth-gutted
    wheat. Two horses lashed to the ends
of a rafter, the drugged circumference
    of their labor turns the machine.
    The man in the hopper
  pushes wheat into a chute, which separates
grain from chaff. A boy clears the waste.
      A shroud of white moths rises
  from his arms.

3.

The thresher's forehead is the color of torn roots, his face
and neck empurpled by sun, spelled only by quick
reshufflings of cirrus.
       He is not
unhappy, only
afflicted by variables. Hail, rust,
          blight, eyespot,
              black chaff,
pink seed, flood, endless depth of sky, endless dark of his bedroom
in which the eye drowns.

4.

      Ornate wallpaper, the smell of cooked meat
like the flush of warmth back
     to a cold extremity:
  women bring bowls
    to the table, men in
  fellowship with men as a reward for labor.
  But for every spotless rack
    of cerulean china
      there is a night
 when the rooster
   conjures a false dawn;
  in its intervals
silence rages in the English garden;
   candle flames like commas
  prolong the dark. This is why
aprons are bleached daily,
why the barn is scrubbed as reclamation from
      scat and sun, why
each man asks for more meat, more labor
   as if bodies
     are made to be consumed.

5.

　　　　To chew the roots of cowbane is a way out. Laudanum under
　　the sink is
a way out. Also, the concept
　　of being a metaphor
　　　　　　for wheat:
　　　　when torn open: raw, prone material
that broken across
a machine or a winter
　　is malleable to
　　　any use.
　　What if they did not want
a way out? Night's oaks swallow wrens, so dark
　　the barn is imperceptible. To sit at that
　　　table emptied of its men is to
learn to take solace in what pours
　　　　　from the window's open mouth.

6.

The last man raises
his face from the bowl. The prairie
    is both hurtling and
  standing still. It will
       not rearrange itself no
      matter how deeply he scrawls his attention
over it. He takes in the thick
    concussions of light.
     He is drawn back to the barn
and past it, where pheasants explode
    from the ditches. He is not hungry
     anymore. Someone will take his seat
at the table. Someone will lower their head
  and ask the Lord to be made
more bare to the sun.
     A clot of moths unravels
across the man's eyes. He asks for no other
    veil over the stillness.
     And the Lord
    provides.

Without You, the Meadow

The cracked light, the pine-slur, the mist.
The black tooth of the dog—the pearl eye of the dog.
The motions of grass in the wind you've become:
wind is what you have become. The blank force
of your face. The crooked silver. The dark.
Not your name but the negative of your name,
not a song but the intensity of song, in the rain.
The raveling. The dog's path, in circles around
the ox. The weight of its yoke—the weight
of its yoke, after the rain, in the barn, taken off.
The neck of the ox, now dry, free, still bent.
The weight nonetheless. The meadow, the same.

The 28th Year

—Unworkable year, X'd out year of woe's third crown,
milk light on a new wife, year of soft burn and touch of blood,
days framed in cracked gilt only to be taken down and stored
somewhere in the lower left corner of the only church

I have ever feared: the barn, toxic and pigeon-zenithed, where,
it seems, all my life lies scattered under the scaffold, tabernacle
of rat, hog chute and cow gallows—one day I will go back and find
my childhood sitting, like it always is, in the silo, waiting

for shadow to trawl down the eclipsed brick to reach him,
signaling it is time to go home; because he measured himself
in this place, standing straight, annual cuts in cedar beams, it will
remain his bibliography;—while here, I measure the sun slice's
slide of annulled yellows down the star-drilled start of sky,
last work of a year aching to rename itself, word one. I see it out.

Curse

Empty field, steeped
in red matrix of sundown,
built like a past: brilliant in wither,
long in purchase; this is land
I inherited. Nitrogen, silk rot,

alfalfa seeds socked in
for the dry burn, is the field's drama.
To stop this slow warp of nostalgia
bending damage and balm
into an unbroken circle is mine. Pitiable

to be as at my fingertips as this field is.
Pitiable how inexhaustible
mist and pig smell are to me.
We owe each other as vowel
and salvation owe each other.

Descent

Gnat-macula in the dark yard, cut throats of fireweed
ooze bitter back to the sinkhole. In a brown recluse's web,
caddis flies hang like a constellation. A twice-removed heir

to hail-stripped crop and soy blight, I trace the field's edge back
towards the house. Corn shivers in its chalk wrap; headlights
sop up the night and roll on. Tonight I'll let drowned farmers
fall like years into my skin. Here where soil performs acts
of reincarnation, is it horror or harvest where hens' blood
champions the grass, or a rash of fox-poached tomcats?

Such slaughter is seasonal, but we do not call it harvest or
horror. These are words for dead farmers, who, in the earth,
intended to be as gentle as this slow blear towards water.

II.

X

Say this firmament—Atlantic, inviolate—holds X amount of rescue.

Shallow in a violent wind, the nerve-drenched voice, *do you know me?*

And full-on in the bleached grass my quenchless need for X to be infinite.

....

Say I don't remember what I was doing in the middle of the corn.

The parallel *S* sounds and the almost subterranean *I* in a violent wind.

This is X? A goose-polluted voice that thralls in the torrent: bray-*do*-bray-*you* . . . ?

....

Say the less-gray tunnel of light in the day's midst is X's nimbus.

As for "Spirit come back eat the mulberries in my yard," what are the mulberries
. like?

Say, in concordance with my quenchlessness, the spirit is my father.

....

The mulberries are black reams of ink, a dissertation on the death of the simile.

Spirit, what is the field like? Composition in pearl, too bright for the Xs of your
eyes?

The gesture "*come back*" is as false as I don't look back.

....

Say cut weeds pepper the pristine yield, the firmament hawked and milky.

(X, forgive me. I look back. I am thirteen years old.)

Rock-fisted, barn windows smashed to glitz, I hate the largess of my parents.

....

Say my father and my grandfather died on the same day.

Holy X of the Perpetual Proof, show me an unbroken circle.

Moonlit alluvium mimics talc, but press your face to it: it is black.

....

Say I evoke the impression of my open-mouthed face in soft earth.

Say I swallowed a dram of soil. When I breathe, I feed the seed of an X tree.

Back acreage scrap-cankered: tire, pipe-splinter, one luminous dishwasher.

....

Say the grown tree of X leaks sap onto the dishwasher, mulberries pox its sheen.

When my father shouldered the machine from the truck, his satisfaction was
                                                                    archaic.

I evoke a violent wind to steal his breath, close his eyes, resume erosion.

....

Damage runs parallel to us: quenchless current in our nerves.

I am in the middle of the corn. I am X years old. Do you know me?

Say I could rescue one luminous field. I steal his eyes. I look back.

Y

Whirr of a .45 ACP. Train-pierced gloss

   of the day's last light.

      The train was our

    river. A heifer,

  acquitted by an anonymous

    boy of her fence

  rocked her dense body

—motion like knuckles rolled

   in the clenched and unclenched

   fist of one who is testing

    the after-pain of

  recoil after re-

   coil, calm the shot-bucked barrel—

past the chapped crops

   and mustered her

  mass onto the tracks. We

     in the farmhouse's hush

    heard the impact of cow

   and train. I went with my father—

she was all

unspooled viscera

and wilderness. She wailed.

In the dark tent of our

attention, we lanterned

by witness.

Or else. I turned.

Echoed cordite reported

a mercy shot.

Z

My father died on the floor of a machine shed on March 4th, 2004, the wind of Illinois
in his lungs.

The wind from Illinois blows backwards across the prairie.
The wind from Illinois moves the wolf-flow south.
The wind from Illinois is an accomplice to drought.
The wind from Illinois burned the chicken coop to ashes.
The wind from Illinois cares nothing about its own.

He was beneath a Chevy Suburban when the jack slipped and its weight was revealed
to him.

The wind from Illinois is the duration of loss.
The wind from Illinois is a plastic curtain to collapse behind.
The wind from Illinois is morphine.
The wind from Illinois is filling a bottle.
I drink to fill the void the wind from Illinois made.

When I found him, a 911 operator spoke a red thread into my ear.

In late winter, the wind from Illinois is a kind of church.
The wind from Illinois is a dome over black elms.
The wind from Illinois points its pale arm and finger.
The wind from Illinois preaches to an audience
of windmills and souls disconnected and spinning wildly.

I stood above him and watched the history of who I was calmly recede.

The wind from Illinois abandons us in favor of endlessness.
A scrap of the wind from Illinois is caught in an empty room.
The wind from Illinois scuttles letters across the floor.
Dearest Sue, tomorrow is already here . . .
The wind from Illinois has no memory.

And now I am outside my history and yet still in the thick roar of the given.

Silo

Citronella-reek in the stray dog necropolis, center chamber
of an unused silo, few stars shining. We, the blister-fingered,
unaccounted-for children burned dry grass in a circle. I imagined
saccharine smoke pooling in the jaws of a colossus we were inside of,
and had sicced ourselves on, tiny horns and little sticks. As my shadow
ascended the wall, I thought of my exile as the Tall Hollow Man.

Ring of silt, ring of ash, bones two feet below: what I caught a glimpse of
was a spirit in butter, an image of a god to be burned in a straw temple.
It's all circumference, familiar light on the china, a divine cipher droning
like white noise in the unstill fields. The sleeve of brick is still here,
no corona, no soot on the loosestrife. I see shadow swallow the room's wicker
and waver, quotidian-creep; white sparks rush to the periphery, and cling.

Of Shade and Body Interwound

All morning, forms have receded in the rain-rinsed cul-de-sac.
The heater shield of the early moon just now hangs up its lone ring.
Today form itself is heroic, anything that pierces nothing's drape
and anti-fury. Like a carousel of lost souls, runners keep coming
back from the dead. 11th hour, you are a terror and I admire you.

Of the Five Enemies today I would invite in Color, eye-salve,
plane of orange, red-pedestaled, yellow-fused. Behind the house,
the original simplicity of man kneels on its grass mat, knowing
as form implies the void, color is mere hood to Undivided Dark.
12th hour, I read you loud and clear. Hide your form, be orderly within.

At the Outermost Shrine of the Narrowmost Road

Black rock, rafts of meadow and a sky of packed ash—
past the dog-shooting grounds, tooth-colored rice,
Hell's Window and Headlong Fall, you come towards the end
of the road you've stuck to, shot shoes and useless suitcase.

You want to lie down in the pigweed's privacy
and know your true place like the salt does, low leech and keeper,
lost hours scattered like dead bees across the sand.
As is, you kneel among the lost bottle-mail of some far quarter,

another sun, another spoke in the wheel of emptiness.
Footprints arrow and meander: this may not be the way,
yet how else to know but take a stormtrue doubt with you, step
into the cold stream, how else to know but through?

Vantage

Backyard in its usual post-moon fade, loll of drugged hostas,
same old piles of detritus held up to the light, spent choke
and St. Augustinegrass. A slow wind endlessly scans the asters
as if for its lost map, white forefinger of the unknown AWOL,
carbon copy salvia shimmer, unoriginal air, yet also Issa's warning:
the world of dew is the world of dew, and yet, and yet . . .

So, from the window I watch for a different light to fall and prove
things otherwise: the curtains shawls of flame, the candle a sibyl,
these boxwoods thousand mile horses. I wait because of the redress
in silence, daring me to open a small tapestry bag of knowledge
and read from the slips of paper what I think I know:
1) Our blood scrolls down the sugar maple 2) Its bark sutures us,
our split skins 3) By fine roots, we are bound home.

Confession

Here, in the oaks' vestral chamber, you can at last say what you
have done. Tell us how you sought the redemptive letter, how
you once tried to interpret prayer as revenge on language, to school
despair into assonance as lead in a vice. Remember the second part
of progress is to shunt muse. Tonight sheep buoy the unreachable blue.
So spirit break your grieve; Master slake your waif. The state
of the accurate world can be illuminating in its disappointments.
4 A.M. eats bits of black air. Of all the stations, you're assigned the last.
Turn toward the vagabond straw, or away, and if away, then go
where none of the others have. Penance does exist. It is out past
the leaves cast lunar in fade, out past the buckshot-peppered silo
and all divided idylls—it is . . . I could to tell you it is attention paid
but it is also a craving. As if one wish can dispel the limits of wish.

Of Love and Wild Dogs

I used to wake early and watch the sheep lift their heads in fear.
Once, a wild dog took shape out of the wood-frost,
slicking its blue tongue, its coat itself a polluted ice,
then hard lunge, gloss of rent muscle, red rash inwound

on the boneyard, no sound, everything disfigured
in mist, everything with its skeleton mask on.
I thought the sheep were meant for hunger, the way
our hunger is meant to become its own guide to call to.

This mist, here, years after, devolves into a mouthful of wool.
I used to want to witness loss, to have my shoeprint in the sheep's
blood be a seal to mark the act as closed. But it is not necessary.
The proof is obliterated by darkening shifts of grass.

I used to wake early and watch a blurred face that came
to be mine flare up in the mirror. Now, in the fallen night,
I can see what is not meant for hunger—throb of stars,
your cool, unwashed skin: trademarks of what rises.

The Imperfect Knowledge of Paolo

Last night the landscape's blue hips sneaked an inch
toward bleak. The clouds were combustible oxen. Francesca,
you never looked so fervently at the antiquity of your hands.
We drifted like synonyms around the root word.

My woman is sometimes in front of me, sometimes behind.
When she is in front, I try to find her attractive. Millennia have glistered
her statuesque features with opal pox. The skein of her beauty
scattered like fractals. When she is behind, I think of apologies to tell her.

I was a pasture of coal. No. You were. There was a time
I would drink your bathwater. Yes: it was worth it.
To have coiled my voice your mouth: yes, your mouth
like a storm, like Hell's, no, a smaller saffron whirlpool of rue.

Is To Say

For my words and their reluctance to rise
for my right hand and its tenebrous circuit its one volt
for the orchard for the hawk helix for the hunt
for the held breath and the loosed note
for the clock's cold soliloquy of numerals
that sighs *recision* to the curtains *recision* to the grey dog
for the dark I enlarge and the light I replace
for the raw grain and shucked skins I've held in my arms
for the road out for the road back
for the X for the X for the X

is *to say*
which is a headache at the back of the mouth
which is to see the whirl of leaves in half-ceded winter
and record it as a felt thing somewhere in the body
a flickering charge of weather a seam of coal in bone
is to trust what can't be trusted
is to conjure with grammar of hawk and clock
but what do you want except for darkness to enlarge
do you want a painting of someone singing
do you want to be that certain

Them Men

We should not be awake.

*

Sark & water   syncopated machine

that is our breath
rocking sixty acres to sleep.

*

Hicksgas Propane   Anhydrous Ammonia

*

Case engine as self-portrait.

A good mechanic

is a connoisseur of the ongoing
conviction that an answer

is forthcoming.

*

On television, all pills are made of light.
Stropped across the screen

the blade of our patience.
A watery sound

like a woman or a pigeon.
From outside?

No. A love scene.

But what was that sound

outside, what was that
strange sound out-
                    side

what

            outside

is not
woman-strange

                or a blade of light?

*

In scrubby ice,
we coax milk

because cows cripple from within
if they do not bestow

all they were made to.

*

We wouldn't know a white gown
from a sheet of field mice

caught in a galvanized bath.

*

The woman in the Snap-on
tools calendar lilts her arms—

a long time passes.

As if she is offering something.

*

As a child,

in the third person,

we stopped time

and spent decades
in the undergrowth.

The straw raged in its tunnel.

III.

Tityrus, there you lie in the beech-tree shade,
Brooding over your music for the Muse,
While we must leave our native place, our homes,
The fields we love, and go elsewhere; meanwhile,
You teach the woods to echo "Amaryllis."

—Meliboeus, from the 1st eclogue of Virgil, trans. David Ferry

Ex Log

Let us begin, Lest

Whose scorching trees
Among snow
Shrivel us back to
The salt story

Gods love threes
The harrowing of a master thirst
Amaryllis
And I

Grant me cave
I will hang
Constellations
Seen by a wolf

Myself Amaryllis
I was entirely still
Your lip bruised
His palest gifts

Love berries
As if with blood
Feed goats
To the world

Amaryllis says
You are the game I
Can never win
Enough

Give Amaryllis
The Argo haircut
Prune the face
Whelm her under

Tamarisk and flint
Devour
This field
With our own eyes

Enough grotto
Vortex
Sterile barley
It's time for two

To placate a calf
Yield all precedence
To its love of
Traps

Boy you
I ambush
Thus
Charm

For blush
A little soot
Easy he is
Already erased

Wanton boy
Speckled with wax
Be quiet
Bequeathed

Him I call
Amaryllis Amaryllis
I call
Home

Bitumen-cast
Ground covered
In his white flank for Amaryllis
And she sees

"What is his name"
Hylas
Fire to hold
You up to

Poison to be all
Cure forgetful to be
All song to be
All-throated god

Behind the hazel
I meet Amaryllis
All flock
Against

We used to murder
Straw women
Come on Amaryllis
We're only halfway killed

"No" Bacchic cornflower
Sirocco-yoked hazel
Cried out
Too

Goat god man
I thrice mimic Pan
Grassfield charmfield
Brokensoldiered

Exit ilex
Amaryllis said no
That face will grieve
When I left me

Twine I
To that which it longs for
Bits of cold
Charge the ground

Bride your maidens men
Cast joy utterly
And when you do
You've fed them

So raise
Your fistful of thorn
Lovely the skin
And lovelier still the vestige

Dogs with
The blood of children
Can be heard
In the events to come

Divisible

Concussions of light.

River, bridge, abandoned mattress.

As if out of need, it is late in the year.

Wolves' bivouac for flense and birth.

Tremble of backwater imperceptible, as when a fever returns.

Too far for me to lay a hand there once or lightly.

All of my errors have been of omission.

I cannot bring a world quite round

Blacksnake armada.

Or is it moccasin.

All of my errors have been of linden.

I cannot bring a word down for the room I left behind.

Poverty of mission.

And other maimed unities.

The room a group of voices has left.

Asphyxiations of wind.

Crawfish odyssey.

A group of voices: myself, brother, mother and.

Omissions, stopped waves.

We will meet at the river.

A wolf placenta stains the abandoned mattress.

Our hour will never come.

Letter Sent in a Fish

How sweet it will be to hand this all back: bent axe,
cinnabarine fire, these hands. Soot fallen by the east gate,
brief path for pheasant & rat: let me become this chopped
and burning pine, to ascend leafless orchards, each wracked singularity
its own sign of failure if we come back to life, which I believe in.
Do you imagine such things? Our prelude over? Hand it back.
And where does it go then? Some uncarved life, a jade badge—
to have it swell in front of me before I must remember this morning,
lice ecstatic in winter sun, far from now, hair drug through blood grass . . .

The rest is as easy as a blind slide and a once round the column:
slipstream, aphid, tiara of moss, buck, mountain that has yet to find the fault
to start its journey; we could come back as any of these. Forget the pine,
let me become a traveler of the river's nadir, bottom-feeder, fugitive,
to know only scum yet be unable not to take it in like sky takes prayer.

Letter Sent Back on a Crane's Heel

A gift swelled from the darkness is to be nailed down.
Light is the instrument. Give to your discontent some work;
pretend you are a realist painter. They know satisfaction.
We are human: humiliation slicks our hair, mercy steers us.
To see, just beyond, perhaps,—promise like a mule in dirge,

the charms around the necks of the dead, road of glory and its
boredom, past dreams of retrieval, beyond the time-to-come we think
might lie behind shadow's plum fever on our windows . . . No, not
a prelude but an Act. To know the world is not to become the world.
Also, the hermit's dream, to be blind and unlooked for, is not our dream.
Let this be ours: the satisfaction of viewing. Do you remember
the crane, invisible in the rushes, until betrayed by its crooked gate,
which led it, inevitably, to a fox-slaughtered crane?
How it lifted, as not away from its mate, but for it?

At the Shade House

Fire is already in your seams. My uncle
is going to burn you down. Asbestos spume
and black up-rushes of matter are already erasing
your roof. Clover drenched in ash.

Henry Roscoe Shade plumbed you in a year of salt.
You were for the farmhands. Grease and straw,
inscrutable men. The whole house spoke
out of the right side of its mouth. You hunkered
shadow-true to the grass. Voles ticked in your margins.
Elms' methodical grief littered your autumns.
Then I came and unloaded one day's worth of teen solitude
by breaking your windows. You were empty.
I would be too smart to be a farmer. I would be
an inscrutable man. I remember the fluency of stone,
crystalline yelps of glass. I memorized each cavity
I made and spent a decade, states away, making more.
Meanwhile men moved in and out of your rooms.
The last I will ever see of your last tenant, tears
in his eyes, at my father's funeral, his hand held
at knee level, meaning *"I have known you since . . ."*
Months later he would charge gasoline
on my father's account at the FS station; my mother
never forgave him. In this winter of your vetted raze,
bats scroll in their broken way across your porch.
I scroll through my gestures of sacrifice, and find
that nothing will do. My uncle scrolls through his
expected dreams of pale corn felled by a noiseless machine
that does not exist, could not, outside of his mind.

My uncle is a man of sticks and cinder.
He will tramp your doused remains.
He is right to do this, I think. You are a house
of silent men. You are carbon in my lungs.

For Tityrus

who had to, as we do now, watch the neighbors leave,
    us from our porch facing Route 45, pollen drifting

like smithereens from some erupted star over the truck
    of a family whose few hundred acres were taken

not grandly by droves of Octavian's godless soldiers
    fresh from civil war, but by simple hard luck, rootworm

and corn borer, too few loans to afford an acrid cascade
    of insecticide dropped from those planes whose tracers

make the mock-girding which fails each night to prop up the sky.
    Tityrus, who purchased in Rome from Octavian himself

the right to continue to graze his flock in the dropped-apple reek of fall
    between the stunted row of tamarisks and the rock outcrop

that marked his land—if he were here I could ask what advice
    to give as they come up the drive to return the twenty yards

of electric fence borrowed to keep raccoons from their pumpkins,
    what to say to this family whose three fields we will soon try to buy

at the lowest negotiable price, so that it won't be our furniture
    someday sticking out the back of a flatbed. Tityrus,

who offered his neighbor one last night in arcadia, clover
    for his sheep, chestnuts and cheese for his journey, did more

than we are willing to. It would take more than generosity
    or condolence to stop this father's belief he's been cheated

by those humid nights spent awake urging on the mass of bats
    constellating above their corn, feeding on that which fled

from our well sprayed land onto theirs, wrecking the yield.
    If Tityrus were standing here with us, watching their exhaust rise,

I would ask him if I should take it as a sign that our farm
    is the last one in the county with its original name, Shadeland,

as night falls and my mind latches on only to that
    which is giving itself over to bare and continuous forces—

the unbeautiful pears fallen at tree's roots, evening wind's
    far off baying, the chipped and gap-bricked mouth of a well

that with each freeze and thaw feeds on itself, increments of stone
    humming beyond earshot into nothing, which is quick, and final.

Shadeland

Beginning with a line from Hopkins

Down roughcast, down dazzling whitewash, wherever an elm arches—
wherever June wind barnstorms the dry stations of barley,
clouds like an old tattoo dragging in rain over the West,
you can almost see how the body moves after life,

fish-tailing across the water hemp, suddenly keen, gunning for any heaven.
Standing in the white pines, their chalk-mail and tin music,
what does this mean to me, starting to fade, even now, hours,
days reshuffling and losing sense in the cipher—

we must work fast: in a pond, somewhere, like a black pearl,
death is spinning itself; memory is the moth turning our anthology
of dead ends to dust above the world of our bodies,
whose skins, in the hoarlight, are frail clay.